INSIDE
THE U.S.A.

INSIDE
THE U.S.A.

NATIONAL GEOGRAPHIC   Hampton-Brown

Acknowledgments

Grateful acknowledgement is given to the authors, artists, photographers, museums, publishers, and agents for permission to reprint copyrighted material. Every effort has been made to secure the appropriate permission. If any omissions have been made or if corrections are required, please contact the Publisher.

Photographs
Cover, Title (tc) Digital Art/Corbis, (l-r) Todd Gipstein/CORBIS, Gerald French/CORBIS, Joseph Sohm/Visions of America/Corbis, Tom Grill/Corbis, Momatiuk – Eastcott/Corbis, Corbis.

Acknowledgments and credits continue on page 101.

Neither the Publisher nor the authors shall be liable for any damage that may be caused or sustained or result from conducting any of the activities in this publication without specifically following instructions, undertaking the activities without proper supervision, or failing to comply with the cautions contained herein.

Published by National Geographic School Publishing & Hampton-Brown
Alison Wagner, President & Chief Executive Officer

The National Geographic Society
John M. Fahey, Jr., President & Chief Executive Officer
Gilbert M. Grosvenor, Chairman of the Board

Manufacturing and Quality Management, The National Geographic Society
Christopher A. Liedel, Executive Vice President & Chief Financial Officer
George Bounelis, Vice President

National Geographic School Publishing
Hampton–Brown
P.O. Box 223220
Carmel, California 93922
www.NGSP.com

Printed in the United States of America

ISBN: 978-0-7362-7055-7

3 4 5 6 7 8 9 10 11 19 18 17 16 15 14 13
HPS232389

Contents

Contents, *continued*

Learning to Read Units 5–6

Learning to Read Units 7–8

Learning to Read Units 9–10

Name _____

High Frequency Words Presentation

LEARN NEW WORDS

 Listen to your teacher.   Say each new word.   Then write it in the boxes.

1. name

Hi, my name is Mona.

2. my

Hello. My name is Pamela.

3. am

I am a new student.

4. I

I live at 24 Main Street.

5. you

You live on my street.

6. is

My home is at 27 Main Street!

Name _____

High Frequency Words Practice

 Read each word aloud. Then write it.

1. am _____ 4. my _____

2. I _____ 5. name _____

3. is _____ 6. you _____

How to Play

1. Make a spinner.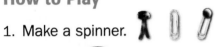

2. Spin.

3. Complete each sentence.

   The first player to complete all six sentences wins.

I _____ Sam.

My name _____ Mat.

See _____ later!

_____ am at school.

This is _____ school.

What is your _____?

Name _____

Letters and Sounds

A. Study the new letters and sounds.

Ss   **Mm**   **Ff**   **Hh**   **Tt**   **Aa**

B. Say the name of each picture below. What letter spells the <u>first</u> sound you hear? Circle the letter.

1.

t (h) a

2.

a h s

3.

h f s

4.

f h a

5.

a m s

6.

t h a

7.

a m t

8.

a s m

9.

t h a

Name _____

Letters and Sounds

Say the name of each picture below. What letter spells the <u>first</u> sound you hear? Write the letter.

1.
_____s_____

2.
_____

3.
_____

4.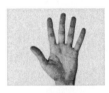
_____

5.
_____

6.
_____

7.
_____

8.
_____

9.
_____

10.
_____

11.
_____

12.
_____

13.
_____

14.
_____

15.
_____

High Frequency Words Presentation

REVIEW HIGH FREQUENCY WORDS

 Read each word aloud. Write the correct word in the sentence.

name	you

is	am

I	My

1. My _____ is Mrs. Martin.

2. I _____ the teacher.

3. _____ like our class.

LEARN NEW WORDS

 Listen to your teacher. Say each new word. Then write it in the boxes.

1. me

My father gave this to me .

m e

2. show

Show me your family.

3. look

You can look at them here.

4. point

Please point to your sister.

5. this

This is my sister.

6. the

The book is very nice.

Name _____

High Frequency Words Practice

 Read each word. Then write it.

1. this _____	4. point _____
2. the _____	5. look _____
3. me _____	6. show _____

1. Find the words. Circle them.

   Look across. ➡

q	t	h	i	s	m
v	k	e	s	l	w
s	b	t	t	h	e
t	l	j	q	t	q
z	p	r	g	m	e
l	o	o	k	q	o
w	f	s	h	o	w
p	o	i	n	t	r

2. Find the words. Circle them.

   Look down. ⬇

m	q	t	j	z	t
e	v	h	u	l	s
k	s	i	r	o	g
o	h	s	p	o	t
r	o	i	o	k	h
x	w	y	i	r	e
w	g	o	n	z	q
p	u	z	t	a	v

 Write the missing words.

1. _____Show_____ me Mexico.
   (Show / This)

2. _____ is a pen.
   (This / Me)

3. Can you help _____?
   (the / me)

4. _____ the book.
   (Read / This)

 Write the missing words.

5. _____ to the
   (Me / Point)
   of the United States.

6. _____ teacher is
   (Read / The)
   from .

Name _____

Words with Short *a*

A. ✏️ Read each word. ✍️ Draw a line to match the word and the picture.

1.
hat

ham

2.
fat

mat

B. ✍️ Write the missing words.

3.

This is a _____hat_____ .

(ham / hat)

6.

I _____ Ron.

(Sam / am)

4.

Maylin is _____ school.

(at / sat)

7.

This is a _____ .

(ham / hat)

5.

Here is the _____ .

(fat / mat)

8.

You _____ at the .

(at / sat)

Name _____

Words with Short *a*

A. Write the missing a. 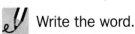 Then read the words aloud in each list.
How are the words different?

1. __a__ m

    S ___ m

    h ___ m

2. ___ t

    h ___ t

    s ___ t

3. ___ t

    f ___ t

    m ___ t

B. What word completes each sentence and tells about the picture?
 Write the word.

4.

Here is my __h__ __a__ __t__ .

5.

I am ___ ___ ___ .

6.

This is a ___ ___ ___ .

7.

I am ___ ___ school.

8.

I ___ ___ Ron.

9.

I ___ ___ ___
on the .

10.

___ ___ ___ a .

11.

Look at the ___ ___ ___ .

12.
I ___ ___ at the ██████ .

13.

You ___ ___ ___ at
the 🪑 .

High Frequency Words Presentation

REVIEW HIGH FREQUENCY WORDS

 Read each word aloud. Write the correct word in the sentence.

this	me

my	am

I	you

1. Ana, _____ is Pat.

2. Pat is _____ brother.

3. Glad to meet _____ .

LEARN NEW WORDS

 Listen to your teacher. Say each new word. Then write it in the boxes.

1. school

Is this my new school ?

 s c h o o l

2. yes

Yes , this is
your new school.

3. it

It is a big school.

4. number

Is this room number 3?

5. no

No , it is not.

6. not

It is not
your classroom.

High Frequency Words Practice

A. 👓 Read each word. ✍ Then write it.

1. number _____	4. not _____
2. it _____	5. school _____
3. no _____	6. yes _____

B. ✍ Write the missing letters.

7. Which words have a **t**?

   __n__ __o__ __t__

   ____ ____

8. Which words have 2 letters?

   ____ ____

   ____ ____

9. Which words have 3 letters?

   ____ ____ ____

   ____ ____

10. Which word ends with **r**?

    ____ ____ ____ ____ ____ ____

11. Which word starts with **s**?

    ____ ____ ____ ____ ____ ____

12. Which words start with an **n**?

    ____ ____ ____ ____ ____

    ____ ____ ____

C. ✍ Write the missing word.

13. This is my ____school____ .
    (school / not)

14. _____ is a small school.
    (No / It)

15. My desk is in room _____ 5.
    (number / yes)

16. It is _____ big.
    (no / not)

17. Is this a pen? ✎

    _____ , it is a pen.
    (Yes / No)

18. Is this a book? 🕐

    _____ , this is not a book.
    (Yes / No)

I AM MAT

FAT SAM

THIS IS MAT.

This is Sam.

SAM IS FAT.

SAM LOOKS AT THE HAM.

NO!

Look at Sam!

SAM HAS MY HAT!

This Is Tam

Tam is fast!

This is Tam.

Look at Tam!

This is the school.

This is the mat.

Tam is at school.

Show me the mat.

Tam has a mat.

Name _____

High Frequency Words Presentation

REVIEW HIGH FREQUENCY WORDS

 Read each word aloud.　 Write the correct word in the sentence.

school	is

Yes	Point

not	name

1. Do you like _____?

2. _____ , I do.

3. I like school, but I do _____ like the food.

LEARN NEW WORDS

 Listen to your teacher.　 Say each new word.　 Then write it in the boxes.

1. **time**

   What 　time　 is it?

2. **at**

   It's 11:30. Lunch is 　at　 noon.

3. **day**

   I bring my lunch from home every 　day　.

4. **what**

   　What　 do you have for lunch today?

5. **tomorrow**

   I have a sandwich. 　Tomorrow　, I will have a taco.

   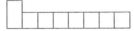

6. **who**

   　Who　 makes your lunch?

High Frequency Words Practice

A. 👓 Read each word. ✍ Then write it.

1. at	_____	4. time	_____
2. day	_____	5. what	_____
3. tomorrow	_____	6. who	_____

B. ✍ Write the missing letters.

7. Which words have 4 letters?

  † i m e
  ___ ___ ___ ___

  ___ ___ ___ ___

8. Which words have an **o**?

  ___ ___ ___

  ___ ___ ___ ___ ___ ___ ___ ___

9. Which word has 2 letters?

  ___ ___

10. Which words have 3 letters?

  ___ ___ ___

  ___ ___ ___

11. Which words have an **a**?

  ___ ___

  ___ ___ ___

  ___ ___ ___

12. Which words have an **h**?

  ___ ___ ___

  ___ ___ ___ ___

C. ✍ Write the missing word.

13. What ____time____ is

  (time / who)

  math class?

14. I have math class

  _____ 10:30.

  (day / at)

15. _____ time is it?

  (Who / What)

16. What _____ do you

  (at / day)

  have P. E.?

17. I have it _____ .

  (day / tomorrow)

18. _____ is

  (Who / Time)

  your teacher?

Letters and Sounds

A. Study the new letters and sounds.

Nn

Ll

Pp

Gg

Ii

B. Say the name of each picture below. What letter spells the <u>first</u> sound you hear? Circle the letter.

1.

   (n)   f   s

2.

   l   p   n

3.

   s   l   n

4.

   t   h   i

5.

   f   m   p

6.

   g   p   l

7.

   p   f   i

8.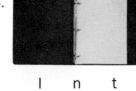

   l   n   t

9.

   l   p   n

10.

   l   g   n

11.

   t   g   a

12.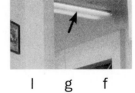

   l   g   f

Letters and Sounds

 Say the name of each picture below. Write the missing letters.

1.

h   a   m

5.

___   i   ___

9.

___   ___   ___

2.

___   ___   ___

6.

m   ___   ___

10.

m   ___   ___

3.

___   i   ___

7.

___   ___   ___

11.

___   i   ___

4.

s   i   ___

8.

___   ___   m   p

12.

___   ___   ___

High Frequency Words Presentation

REVIEW HIGH FREQUENCY WORDS

 Read each word aloud. Write the correct word in the sentence.

Look	What

am	is

my	I

1. _____ is on the table?

2. It _____ a book.

3. Is it _____ book?

LEARN NEW WORDS

 Listen to your teacher. Say each new word. Then write it in the boxes.

1. play

Can you **play** soccer?

2. can

Yes, I **can** play very well!
I play soccer in P. E. class.

3. that

That sport is my favorite.

4. write

My favorite class is ESL.
I learn to **write** in English.

5. read

I learn to **read** .

6. answer

When the ESL teacher asks a
question, I know the **answer** !

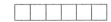

High Frequency Words Practice

A. Read each word. Then write it.

1. can	_____	4. write	_____
2. play	_____	5. read	_____
3. that	_____	6. answer	_____

B. Write the missing letters.

7. Which words have 4 letters?

   p   l   a   y

   ___   ___   ___   ___

   ___   ___   ___   ___

8. Which word has an **i**?

   ___   ___   ___   ___   ___

9. Which word has 3 letters?

   ___   ___   ___

10. Which word starts with an **r**?

   ___   ___   ___   ___

11. Which word has an **l**?

   ___   ___   ___   ___

12. Which word starts with **a**?

   ___   ___   ___   ___   ___   ___

C. Write the missing word.

13. When do you _____play_____ soccer?
                            (can / play)

14. I _____ play it in P. E.
                (can / write)

15. _____ sounds like fun.
           (Answer / That)

16. I _____ in English.
                (that / read)

17. I _____ in English, too.
                (write / that)

18. I got the right _____ .
                (answer / play)

Words with Short *a* and *i*

A. Read each word. Draw a line to match the word and the picture.

1.

pan

map

man

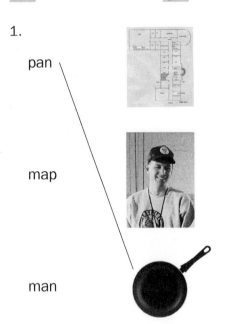

2.

pin

sit

pig

B. Write the missing words.

3.

She has a
___hat___ .
(hat / mat)

5.

This is a
_____ .
(fan / man)

7.

This is a
_____ .
(pin / pig)

9.

This is a
_____ .
(pan / pig)

4.

This is a
_____ .
(pan / ham)

6.

_____ it!
(Pin / Hit)

8.

He is a
_____ .
(man / mat)

10.

You
_____
(sit / hit)

in a .

Words with Short *a* and *i*

A.  Write the missing letters.  Then read the words in each list. How are the words different?

1.
 h __ __

 __ __ __

 __ __ __

2.
 p __ __

 __ __ __

 __ __ __

B. 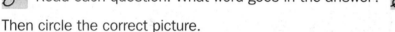 Read each question. What word goes in the answer?  Write the word.

Then circle the correct picture.

3. Where is the pig?

The __p__ __i__ __g__ is here.

4. Where is the pan?

Here is the __ __ __ .

5. Where is Sam?

__ __ __ is at school.

6. Who hit it?

Carlos __ __ __ it.

7. Who has the hat?

She __ __ __ the hat.

8. Who is the man?

He is the __ __ __ .

High Frequency Words Presentation

REVIEW HIGH FREQUENCY WORDS

 Read each word aloud. Write the correct word in the sentence.

what	day

it	play

show	can

1. It's a beautiful _____ today.

2. Yes, we can _____ baseball.

3. Or we _____ play soccer.

LEARN NEW WORDS

 Listen to your teacher. Say each new word. Then write it in the boxes.

1. boy

Who is that boy ?

2. he

That is Jamal. **He** plays soccer well.

3. girl

That **girl** plays well, too.

4. she

Yes. **She** is Jamal's cousin.

5. they

They are good!

6. we

We like to watch them play.

Name _____

High Frequency Words Practice

A. 👓 Read each word. ✏️ Then write it.

1. he	_____	4. they	_____
2. she	_____	5. boy	_____
3. we	_____	6. girl	_____

B. ✏️ Write the missing letters.

7. Which words have 3 letters?

  b   o   y

  ___ ___ ___

8. Which word has an **i**?

  ___ ___ ___ ___

9. Which words have 2 letters?

  ___ ___

  ___ ___

10. Which words have 4 letters?

  ___ ___ ___ ___

  ___ ___ ___ ___

C. ✏️ Write the missing word.

11. Marta is a ____girl____ .
  (boy / girl)

12. _____ is a girl in my class.
  (She / He)

13. Raúl is a _____ .
  (boy / girl)

14. _____ is a boy in my class.
  (She / He)

15. _____ speak two languages.
  (We / Boy)

16. _____ speak one language.
  (They / He)

Read On Your Own
FIN FLIP

TIM HAS A SLIP.

TIM IS ON THE LIST.

☑ BEN
☑ SANDY
☑ CARL
☑ SACHI
☑ TIM
☐ LIN
☐ STEVE
☐ ROBERTA
☐ GORD

TIM AND LIN SIT. LIN HAS A PASS.

Tim, pin it on.

TIM IS IN.

ZOO

This can hiss.

The fish has gills and fins.

FLIP!

IT FLIPS A FIN AT TIM!

Read On Your Own

TIM SLIPS

TIM FILLS A GLASS.

TIM SIPS.

TIM WALKS. TIM STILL SIPS.

TIM SLIPS! THE GLASS SPILLS.

THE GLASS SPILLS ON LIN'S LIST.

LIN HAS A TIP.

Tim, sit if you sip.

Tim and Lil

Lil can play!

This is Tim at school.

This is it!

This is Lil. She sits at school.

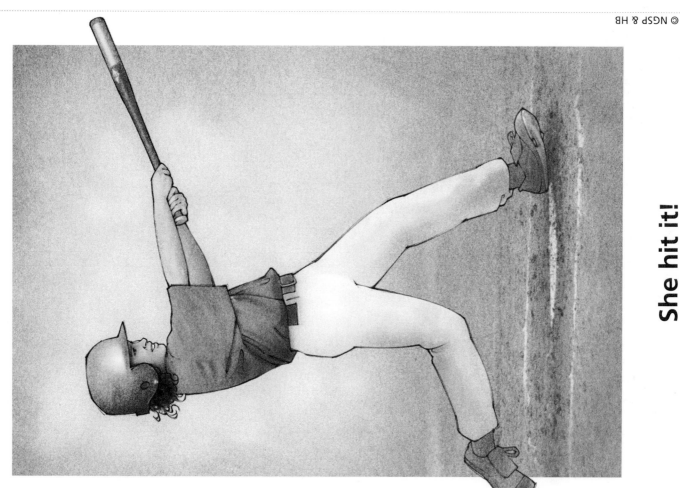

She hit it!

It is 3:00 o'clock.

Tim has a mitt.

Lil has a bat.

High Frequency Words Presentation

REVIEW HIGH FREQUENCY WORDS

 Read each word aloud. Write the correct word in the sentence.

what	at

she	my

time	tomorrow

1. Is Anna _____ school?

2. No , _____ is not.

3. Call her _____ .

LEARN NEW WORDS

 Listen to your teacher. Say each new word. Then write it in the boxes.

1. food

This place makes the best **food** .

 f o o d

2. are

Yes. These tacos **are** delicious.

3. some

Try **some** chips and salsa.

4. of

Do you want a bowl **of** fruit?

5. an

No, thanks. I'll just have **an** apple.

6. a

I'll have **a** big dessert.

High Frequency Words Practice

 Read each word aloud. 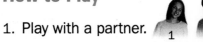 Then write it.

1. an _____   4. a _____

2. of _____   5. some _____

3. are _____   6. food _____

How to Play

1. Play with a partner. Each partner chooses a sign. X O

2. Partner 1 reads a word and marks the square with a sign.

3. Partner 2 takes a turn.

4. Get 3 X s or O s in a row to win.

A.

an	food	a
some	of	are
she	we	he

C.

a	he	we
food	some	an
of	she	are

B.

some	they	an
girl	are	boy
of	food	a

D.

boy	are	of
food	an	girl
they	a	some

Name _____

Letters and Sounds

A. Study the new letters and sounds.

Rr   **Dd**   **Cc**   **Vv**   **Oo**

B. Say the name of each picture below. What letter spells the <u>first</u> sound you hear? Circle the letter.

1.
   m   (d)   o

5.
   c   n   v

9.
   r   d   f

13.
   c   p   t

2.
   r   v   n

6.
   o   r   i

10.
   a   v   l

14.
   o   m   v

3.
   l   h   c

7.
   l   g   c

11.
   d   a   s

15.
   o   d   i

4.
   a   r   d

8.
   h   t   p

12.
   v   i   h

16.
   d   g   v

Name _____

Letters and Sounds

 Say the name of each picture below. Write the missing letters.

1.

   d   o   t

2.

   ___ ___ ___

3.

   ___ o ___

4.

   ___ ___ ___

5.

   ___ ___ ___

6.

   f l ___ ___

7.

   c l ___ s s

8.

   ___ a ___

9.

   ___ a ___

10.

    ___ ___ m p

11.

    ___ ___ ___

12.

    ___ ___ ___

High Frequency Words Presentation

REVIEW HIGH FREQUENCY WORDS

 Read each word aloud. Write the correct word in the sentence.

| This   Show | 1. _____ is my friend.

| name   day | 2. His _____ is Eric.

| He   They | 3. _____ is from Kenya.

LEARN NEW WORDS

 Listen to your teacher. Say each new word. Then write it in the boxes.

1. don't

I don't like bananas.

2. these

Look at these oranges.

3. like

Do you like oranges?

4. and

Yes, I like oranges and apples.

5. those

Then buy these oranges and those apples.

6. good

The apple tastes really good.

High Frequency Words Practice

A. 🗨 Read each word aloud. ✍ Then write it.

1. like _____	4. and _____
2. these _____	5. good _____
3. don't _____	6. those _____

B. ✍ Write the missing letters.

7. Which word has 3 letters?

<u>a</u> <u>n</u> <u>d</u>

8. Which words have an **s**?

____ ____ ____ ____ ____

____ ____ ____ ____ ____

9. Which word ends in **t**?

____ ____ ____ ____

10. Which words have 4 letters?

____ ____ ____ ____

____ ____ ____ ____

____ ____ ____ ____

11. Which word starts with **l**?

____ ____ ____ ____

12. Which words end in **d**?

____ ____ ____

____ ____ ____ ____

C. ✍ Write the missing word.

13. This soup is _____<u>good</u>_____.
   (good / these)

14. I _____ eat lunch
   (and / don't)
   in the cafeteria.

15. _____ are my friends.
   (Good / Those)

16. Give _____ bananas
   (like / these)
   to them.

17. Do you _____ pizza?
   (like / those)

18. I like pizza _____ tacos.
   (and / don't)

Name _____

Words with Short *a*, *i*, and *o*

A. Read each word. Draw a line to the correct picture.

1.

sit

map

man

2.

pan

pig

pin

3.

dot

pot

mop

B. Write the missing words.

4.

This is a

___van___ .

(van / man)

5.

I like this

_____ .

(map / man)

6.

The _____
      (pot / dot)
is hot.

7.

Here is a good

_____ .

(map / mop)

8.

This is a

_____ .

(not / dot)

9.

This lamp is

_____ .

(am / on)

Name _____

Words with Short *a*, *i*, and *o*

A. ✍ Write the missing letters. 💬 Then read the words aloud in each list. How are the words different?

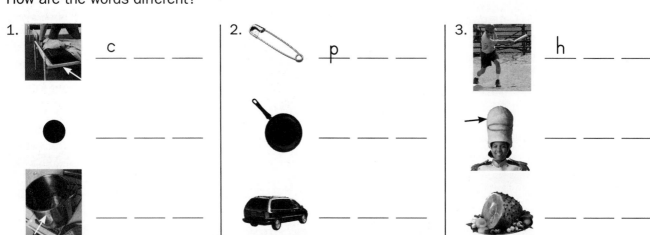

1. c __ __
    __ __ __
    __ __ __

2. p __ __
    __ __ __
    __ __ __

3. h __ __
    __ __ __
    __ __ __

B. ✂ Read each question and the answer. ✍ Write the missing words. Then circle the correct picture.

4. Is this pot hot?

   No, the __p_ _o_ _t_ is not __h_ _o_ _t_.

5. Is this your cap?

   Yes, it is my ____ ____ ____ .

6. Where is the mop?

   The ____ ____ ____ is here.

7. Where can I sit?

   You can ____ ____ ____ here.

8. Where is the dot?

   The ____ ____ ____ is here!

   ✓   ●

9. Do you like the hat?

   Yes, I like the ____ ____ ____ .

High Frequency Words Presentation

REVIEW HIGH FREQUENCY WORDS

 Read each word aloud. Write the correct word in the sentence.

My	This

1. _____ is fun.

are	it

2. Yes, _____ is!

play	at

3. Let's _____ again.

LEARN NEW WORDS

 Listen to your teacher. Say each new word. Then write it in the boxes.

1. do

What do you need?

d o

2. book

I need one more book .

3. does

What does it look like?

4. picture

It has a picture of 3 dogs on it.

5. both

Here it is! Do you want both books?

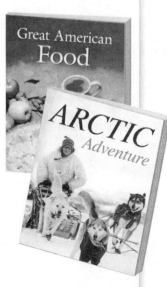
Great American Food

ARCTIC Adventure

6. How

Yes. How much are they?

Name _____

High Frequency Words Practice

A. 🗨 Read each word aloud. ✍ Then write it.

1. does _____	4. picture _____
2. how _____	5. book _____
3. both _____	6. do _____

B. ✍ Write the missing letters.

7. Which words have 4 letters?

d __ o __ e __ s __

___ ___ ___ ___

___ ___ ___ ___

8. Which words start with **d**?

___ ___

___ ___ ___ ___

9. Which word ends with **w**?

___ ___ ___

10. Which word has an **i**?

___ ___ ___ ___ ___ ___ ___

11. Which words start with **b**?

___ ___ ___ ___

___ ___ ___ ___

12. Which word has two **o**'s?

___ ___ ___ ___

C. ✍ Write the missing word.

13. Look at this ____book____ .
(do / book)

14. I like the _____ on it.
(both / picture)

15. _____ much is it?
(How / Does)

16. _____ it cost five dollars?
(Does / Do)

17. _____ you want this
(Does / Do)
book, too?

18. I want _____ books.
(how / both)

© NGSP & HB

Read On Your Own

HOT SOUP

Read On Your Own

MOP TIME

Dot and Ron

Dot hops on the beam.

Ron hops off.
He is on the mat.

Ron hops on the rings.

Dot hops off.
She is on the mat.

Look at Dot!

Look at Ron!

High Frequency Words Presentation

REVIEW HIGH FREQUENCY WORDS

 Read each word aloud. Write the correct word in the sentence.

How	That

day	like

don't	does

1. _____ food looks good.

2. I don't _____ milk.

3. Then _____ drink it.

LEARN NEW WORDS

 Listen to your teacher. Say each new word. Then write it in the boxes.

1. old

My shoes are **old**.

o	l	d

2. has

This shoe **has** a hole in it.
My foot is cold!

3. get

I need to **get** new shoes.

4. call

I will **call** the shoe store.

5. have

Now I **have** new shoes.

6. great

My new shoes
are **great**!

High Frequency Words Practice

A. 👀 Read each word. ✍️ Then write it.

1. have	_____	4. old	_____	
2. call	_____	5. great	_____	
3. has	_____	6. get	_____	

B. ✍️ Write the missing letters.

7. Which words have 3 letters?

   _o_   _l_   _d_

   ___   ___   ___

   ___   ___   ___

8. Which words have an **e**?

   ___   ___   ___

   ___   ___   ___   ___

   ___   ___   ___   ___   ___

9. Which words have 4 letters?

   ___   ___   ___   ___

   ___   ___   ___   ___

10. Which word has 5 letters?

   ___   ___   ___   ___   ___

11. Which word ends with a **d**?

   ___   ___   ___

C. ✍️ Write the missing word.

12. She ____has____ brown hair.
    (has / old)

13. I _____ long hair.
    (have / has)

14. My hairstyle is _____ .
    (get / old)

15. I will _____ my mother.
    (call / great)

16. I will _____ a hair cut.
    (get / old)

17. It will look _____ .
    (has / great)

Name _____

Letters and Sounds

 Study the new letters and sounds.

Jj   **Bb**   **Ww**   **Kk**   **Ee**

How to Play Bingo

1. 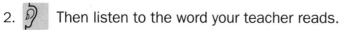 Write the letters from the box. Write one letter in each square.

2. Then listen to the word your teacher reads.

3. Put a ◯ on the letter that stands for the first sound in the word.

4. The first player to cover all the letters in a row is the winner.

Letters to Write

a	i	p
b	j	r
b	j	s
c	k	t
d	k	v
e	l	w
f	m	w
g	n	
h	o	

Words to Read

am	got	lot	top
bat	hit	mat	van
big	it	not	wig
can	jam	on	win
dot	jog	pin	
egg	kid	red	
fat	kit	sit	

Letters and Sounds

 Say the name of each picture below. Write the missing letters.

1.

p o t

2.

___ ___ ___

3.

___ ___ ___

4.

___ g g

5.

___ e s t

6.

___ ___ ___

7.

___ ___ ___

8.

___ o g

9.

___ ___ i g

10.

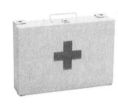

___ i t

11.

___ e ___

12.

___ e ___ ___

Name _____

High Frequency Words Presentation

REVIEW HIGH FREQUENCY WORDS

 Read each word aloud. Write the correct word in the sentence.

are	look

has	am

have	read

1. Hello. How _____ you?

2. I _____ fine.

3. I _____ a headache.

LEARN NEW WORDS

 Listen to your teacher. Say each new word. Then write it in the boxes.

1. **feel**

   How do you feel ?

    f e e l

2. **very**

   I am very sick.

3. **too**

   I feel tired, too .

4. **your**

   Put this in your mouth.

5. **things**

   Do these things when you get home.

   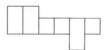

6. **put**

   Put a cold towel on your head. Drink water. Rest in bed.

High Frequency Words Practice

A. 👀 Read each word. ✍ Then write it.

1. feel	_____	4. too	_____
2. put	_____	5. things	_____
3. very	_____	6. your	_____

B. ✍ Write the missing letters.

7. Which words have an **r**?

<u>y</u>   <u>o</u>   <u>u</u>   <u>r</u>

___   ___   ___   ___

8. Which words have 3 letters?

___   ___   ___

___   ___   ___

9. Which words have 4 letters?

___   ___   ___   ___

___   ___   ___   ___

___   ___   ___   ___

10. Which word has 6 letters?

___   ___   ___   ___   ___

C. ✍ Write the missing word.

11. How do you ____feel____ ?
(feel / too)

12. I feel _____ sick.
(things / very)

13. I feel bad, _____ .
(too / your)

14. Take your _____ when you
(very / things)
go home.

15. I _____ them on
(put / feel)
the table.

16. Don't forget _____ bag.
(your / put)

Words with Short *a, i, o,* and *e*

A.  Read each word. Draw a line to the correct picture.

1.
jam

ham

hat
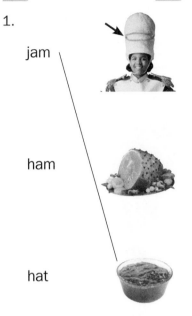

2.
pen

ten

men

3.
cat

bat

bed

B. Write the missing words.

4.

Here are two
_____men_____ .
(men / ten)

5.

There are
_____ dots.
(ten / pen)

6.
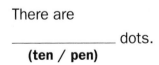
My pet is a
_____ .
(pig / pin)

7.
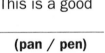
This is a good
_____ .
(pan / pen)

8.
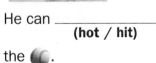
He can _____
(hot / hit)
the ⚪ .

9.
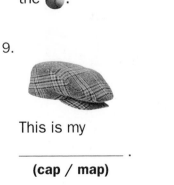
This is my
_____ .
(cap / map)

10.

Here is a
_____ .
(bed / Ed)

11.
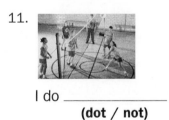
I do _____
(dot / not)
like to play.

12.
Put it in the
_____ .
(pot / pat)

Words with Short *a*, *i*, *o*, and *e*

A. Write the missing letters. 💬 Then read the words aloud in each list.
How are the words different?

1. m ___ ___ ___

 ___ ___ ___

 ___ ___ ___

2. c ___ ___ ___

 ___ ___ ___

 ___ ___ ___

3. p ___ ___

 ___ ___ ___

 ___ ___ ___

B.  Write the missing letters.

4.

This is my __p__ __e__ __n__ .

5.

Look at the
___ ___ ___ .

6.

Here is my
___ ___ ___ .

7.

Carlos has a
___ ___ ___ .

8.

Do you like my
___ ___ __s__ __t__ ?

9.

This is a
__f__ __l__ ___ .

10.

I like to ___ ___ ___ .

11.

I ___ ___ ___ at my
___ ___ ___ ___ .

12.

Where is my
___ ___ ___ ?

High Frequency Words Presentation

REVIEW HIGH FREQUENCY WORDS

 Read each word aloud. Write the correct word in the sentence.

| has   have |
| Does   Do |
| and   too |

1. I _____ my books.

2. _____ you have a pen?

3. Yes. I have paper, _____ .

LEARN NEW WORDS

 Listen to your teacher.   Say each new word. Then write it in the boxes.

1. help

I need your help .

2. group

A group of my friends will come.

3. with

Can you work with us?

4. need

We need to put things in boxes.

5. little

We have big and little boxes.

6. them

We will put them on a truck.

Name _____

High Frequency Words Practice

A. 👓 Read each word. ✍ Then write it.

1. little _____   4. them _____

2. help _____   5. with _____

3. group _____   6. need _____

B. ✍ Write the missing letters.

7. Which words have 4 letters?

t   h   e   m

___ ___ ___ ___

___ ___ ___ ___

8. Which word has a **w**?

___ ___ ___ ___

9. Which words have an **e**?

___ ___ ___ ___

___ ___ ___ ___

___ ___ ___ ___

10. Which words have a **p**?

___ ___ ___ ___

___ ___ ___ ___

C. ✍ Write the missing word.

11. I ____need____ to get directions.
(little / need)

12. I will give _____ to you.
(with / them)

13. Thanks, these will _____ .
(help / with)

14. My house has a _____ garden.
(with / little)

15. I will bring my friends _____ me.
(with / them)

16. It will be a fun _____ .
(group / need)

58 Practice Book

© NGSP & HB

Read On Your Own

GET IN BED, KEN

Read On Your Own

PEG and MEG

Help me get a dress, Peg.

Get this, Meg.

No. Not a red dress.

DRESS TWO....

Meg?

No. It is a wet net with a belt.

DRESS SEVEN....

No, Peg. It is very short and I have long legs.

DRESS TEN....

YES! This is the best!

Tell me you will get it, Meg.

Good! I get to rest!

Where Is My Pen?

Now my face is red!

High Frequency Words Presentation

REVIEW HIGH FREQUENCY WORDS

 Read each word aloud. Write the correct word in the sentence.

is	are

1. The post office _____ across the street.

with	need

2. What do you _____ ?

them	these

3. I need to mail _____ letters.

LEARN NEW WORDS

 Listen to your teacher. Say each new word. Then write it in the boxes.

1. on

I live | on | second street.

| o | n |

2. where

| Where | do you live?

3. around

I live | around | the corner, on Fifth Avenue.

4. work

But I | work | at 44 Elm Street, near the park.

5. take

I | take | the bus to get there.

6. give

I drive by there.
I will | give | you a ride.

High Frequency Words Practice

A. 👓 Read each word. ✎ Then write it.

1. give	_____	4. work	_____
2. take	_____	5. around	_____
3. on	_____	6. where	_____

B. ✎ Write the missing letters.

7. Which word ends with an **e**?

w   h   e   r   e
___ ___ ___ ___ ___

___ ___ ___ ___

8. Which words have a **w**?

___ ___ ___ ___ ___

___ ___ ___ ___

9. Which word has 6 letters?

___ ___ ___ ___ ___ ___

10. Which word has 2 letters?

___ ___

C. ✎ Write the missing word.

11. ____Where____ is the library?
    (Around / Where)

12. The library is _____
    (take / on)
    the right.

13. I will _____ this book.
    (take / work)

14. I will look _____ for an
    (give / around)
    empty table.

15. I can _____ you my book.
    (give / where)

16. Thanks, that will help with my

    _____ .
    (around / work)

Letters and Sounds

 Study the new letters and sounds.

Zz

Yy

Uu

Qq

Xx

How to Play Bingo

1. Write the letters from the box. Write one letter in each square.

2. Then listen to the word your teacher reads.

3. Put a ◯ on the letter that stands for the first sound in the word.

4. The first player to cover all the letters in a row is the winner.

Letters to Write

a	j	s
b	k	t
c	l	u
d	m	v
e	n	w
f	o	y
g	p	z
h	q	
i	r	

Words to Read

am	him	on	van
bat	in	pen	wig
cot	jam	quit	yes
dot	kid	red	zip
egg	lot	sat	
fan	map	ten	
got	not	up	

Name _____

Letters and Sounds

 Say the name of each picture below. Write the missing letters.

1.

l e g

2.

___ ___ i l t

3.

___ ___

4.

___ ___ ___

5.

___ ___ ___

6.

___ ___ ___ ___

7.

___ u ___

8.

___ u ___

9.

___ ___

10.

___ ___ ___

11.

___ u ___

12.

___ ___ ___

High Frequency Words Presentation

REVIEW HIGH FREQUENCY WORDS

 Read each word aloud.　 Write the correct word in the sentence.

has	have

answer	need

they	them

1. Will you _____ a party?

2. I asked my parents, but I didn't get an _____.

3. Ask _____ again.

LEARN NEW WORDS

 Listen to your teacher.　 Say each new word.　 Then write it in the boxes.

1. to

I am going **to** study for
our history test.

t	o

2. which

Which dates do we need to know?

3. here

Look **here** , in your
notebook.

4. in

The important dates are here
in your notes. Study them.

5. letters

Every day, I write the **letters**
and words I learn.

6. will

I **will** write my answers on the test.
I hope they are correct!

High Frequency Words Practice

A. 👁 Read each word. ✍ Then write it.

1. in	_____	4. here	_____
2. to	_____	5. will	_____
3. letters	_____	6. which	_____

B. ✍ Write the missing letters.

7. Which words have an **e**?

<u>l</u> <u>e</u> <u>t</u> <u>t</u> <u>e</u> <u>r</u> <u>s</u>

___ ___ ___ ___

8. Which words have an **i**?

___ ___

___ ___ ___ ___

___ ___ ___ ___ ___

9. Which words have a **t**?

___ ___

___ ___ ___ ___ ___ ___ ___

10. Which words have 2 letters?

___ ___

___ ___

C. ✍ Write the missing word.

11. I am going _____to_____ the
    (to / here)
    shoe store.

12. I _____ buy a pair of shoes.
    (will / which)

13. _____ shoes will you buy?
    (In / Which)

14. They have _____ on
    (will / letters)
    the side.

15. Can you get them _____ ?
    (here / which)

16. Let's go _____ the store
    (in / letters)
    and see.

Name _____

Words with Short *a*, *i*, *o*, *e*, and *u*

A. Read each word. Draw a line to the correct picture.

1.
cot

cat

cap

2.
up

cup

cut

3.
ax

ox

box

B.  Say the name of each picture below. Write the missing letters.

4.

I can __z__ __i__ __p__ it.

6.

I like this old

____ ____ ____ ____ ____ .

8.

I have ____ ____ ____ pins.

5.

This is my ____ ____ ____ .

7.

Do you like my little

____ ____ ____ ?

9.

Is this a pig?

____ ____ ____ !

Name _____

Words with Short *a*, *i*, *o*, *e*, and *u*

A. Write the missing letters. Then read the words in each list. How are the words different?

1.

<u>u</u> <u>p</u>

_ _ _

_ _ _

2.

c _ _

_ _ _

_ _ _

3.

p _ _

_ _ _

_ _ _

B.  Write the missing letters.

4.

There is <u>m</u> <u>i</u> <u>l</u> <u>k</u> in my _ _ _ .

5.

Is this my _ _ _ ?

6.

He _ _ _ it.

7.

_ _ _ _ _ .

8.

She can _ _ _ it.

9.

He has an _ _ _ .

10.

There is a bug on my _ _ _ .

11.

Here is an _ _ .

12.

The lamp is not in the _ _ _ .

High Frequency Words Presentation

REVIEW HIGH FREQUENCY WORDS

 Read each word aloud. Write the correct word in the sentence.

Tomorrow	Day

1. _____ is the last day of school!

is	will

2. What _____ you do this summer?

help	give

3. I will _____ my mother at the store.

LEARN NEW WORDS

 Listen to your teacher. Say each new word. Then write it in the boxes.

1. night

In the winter, | night | comes early.

 n i g h t

2. think

Yes, I | think | summer is better.

3. later

I like it when night comes | later |.

4. for

Summer is better | for | baseball.

5. see

Yes. You don't need the lights to | see | the ball.

6. soon

It will be summer again | soon |. I can't wait.

7. year

It is the best time of the | year |.

Name _____

High Frequency Words Practice

A. ✏ Read each word. ✎ Then write it.

1. see	_____	5. night	_____
2. later	_____	6. think	_____
3. soon	_____	7. year	_____
4. for	_____		

B. ✎ Write the missing letters.

8. Which words have 5 letters?

t   h   i   n   k
___ ___ ___ ___ ___

___ ___ ___ ___ ___

9. Which words have an **i**?

___ ___ ___ ___ ___

___ ___ ___ ___ ___

10. Which words have an **o**?

___ ___ ___

___ ___ ___

11. Which words have an **e**?

___ ___ ___

___ ___ ___ ___

___ ___ ___ ___ ___

C. ✎ Write the missing word.

12. I will visit my friends this

_____year_____ .
   (year / for)

13. I hope to see them _____ .
   (soon / night)

14. I _____ they are a
   (later / think)
lot of fun.

15. At _____ , they ride a bus
   (soon / night)
to the movies.

16. I like to _____ them.
   (year / see)

17. I haven't seen them _____
   (see / for)
two months.

18. I have to go, but I will call you

_____ .
   (later / think)

Read On Your Own
Summer Fun

NAN HAS FUN WITH HER PUP, BUD.

BUD SEES A BUG. HE JUMPS.

BUD SEES A BUS. HE RUNS.

NAN AND BUD RUN UP THE HILL.

NAN HUGS BUD AS THE SUN SETS.

NAN HAS A HOT DOG IN A BUN.

It is not for you.

THEN THEY REST ON A RUG.

Read On Your Own

When Can I Have Fun?

Where Is the Sun?

At last, Jan has fun in the sun.

There is no sun. This is no fun for Jan.

Here it is!

Jan will look for the sun.

Jan looks up a book.

Jan gets on the bus.

Jan runs up the steps.

S	S	S	S	S
M	M	M	M	M
F	F	F	F	F
H	H	H	H	H
T	T	T	T	T
A	A	A	A	A

s	s	s	s	s
m	m	m	m	m
f	f	f	f	f
h	h	h	h	h
t	t	t	t	t
a	a	a	a	a

N	N	N	N	N
L	L	L	L	L
P	P	P	P	P
G	G	G	G	G
I	I	I	I	I

n	n	n	n	n
l	l	l	l	l
p	p	p	p	p
g	g	g	g	g
i	i	i	i	i

R	R	R	R	R
D	D	D	D	D
C	C	C	C	C
V	V	V	V	V
O	O	O	O	O

r	r	r	r
d	d	d	d
c	c	c	c
v	v	v	v
o	o	o	o

J	J	J	J	J
B	B	B	B	B
W	W	W	W	W
K	K	K	K	K
E	E	E	E	E

j	j	j	j	j
b	b	b	b	b
w	w	w	w	w
k	k	k	k	k
e	e	e	e	e

Z	Z	Z	Z	Z
Y	Y	Y	Y	Y
Qu	Qu	Qu	Qu	Qu
X	X	X	X	X
U	U	U	U	U

z z z z z

y y y y y

qu qu qu qu qu

x x x x x

u u u u u

Yes	School	Not	No
It	Number	Show	Look
Point	Me	The	This
You	Name	My	
Is	I	Am	

yes	it	point		
school	number	me	you	is
not	show	the	name	I
no	look	this	my	am

© NGSP & HB

Girl	Boy	They	We
She	He	Answer	Read
Write	That	Play	Can
Who	What	Time	
Tomorrow	Day	At	

girl	boy	they	we
she	he	answer	read
write	that	play	can
	who	what	time
	tomorrow	day	at

Both	Does	Do	Book
Picture	How	These	Good
Don't	Those	Like	And
An	A	Are	
Of	Some	Food	

© NGSP & HB

both

picture

don't

does

how

those

an

of

do

these

like

a

some

book

good

and

are

food

Need	With	Them	Group
Help	Little	Your	Things
Too	Very	Put	Feel
Get	Great	Old	
Has	Call	Have	

need	with	them	group
help	little	your	things
too	very	put	feel
	get	great	old
	has	call	have

Year	Think	Night	For
Soon	Later	See	Which
Will	Here	Letters	To
In	Where	Around	Work
On	Take		Give

year	soon	will	in	
think	later	here	where	on
night	see	letters	around	take
for	which	to	work	give

Photographs:

1 (tl) Elea Dumas/Nonstock/jupiterimages, (bl) Radius Images/jupiterimages, (br) Elea Dumas/Nonstock/jupiterimages. **3** Row 1: (l, lml) PhotoDisc/Getty Images, (ml) Digital Stock, (mr, rmr) PhotoDisc/Getty Images, (r) Artville. Row 2: (l) Ryan McVay/Getty Images, (m) Digital Stock, (r) Metaphotos. Row 3: (l) LWA/Getty Images, (m) Harald Sund/Getty Images, (r) PhotoDisc/Getty Images. Row 4: (l) Steve Cole/Getty Images, (m) Paul Beard/Getty Images, (r) PhotoDisc/Getty Images. **4** Row 1: (l, m) PhotoDisc/Getty Images, (r) Paul Beard/Getty Images. Row 2: (l) PhotoDisc/Getty Images, (m) EyeWire, (r) Digital Stock. Row 3: (l) PhotoDisc/Getty Images, (m) Metaphotos, (r) PhotoDisc/Getty Images. Row 4: (l, m) Digital Stock, (r) PhotoDisc/Getty Images. Row 5: (l) Artville, (m) Steve Cole/Getty Images, (r) PhotoDisc/Getty Images. **5** (l) Gabe Palmer/CORBIS, (r) Design Pics Inc/Alamy. **6** (l) Corbis/jupiterimages, (r) PhotoDisc/Getty Images. **7** Row 1: (l) Artville, (r) Lancelot/Photononstop/Photolibrary.com. Row 2: (l) Ron Chapple Stock/Photolibrary.com, (r) Liz Garza Williams. Row 3: (l) Ron Chapple Stock/Photolibrary.com, (r) Getty Images. Row 4: (l) Getty Images, (r) Artville. Row 5: (l) Liz Garza Williams, (r) White Packert/Getty Images. **8** Row 1: (l) Ron Chapple Stock/Photolibrary.com, (r) Liz Garza Williams. Row 2: (l) Lancelot/Photononstop/Photolibrary.com, (r) Liz Garza Williams. Row 3: (l) Artville, (r) Liz Garza Williams. Row 4: (l) Getty Images, (r) Liz Garza Williams. Row 5: (l) Getty Images, (r) White Packert/Getty Images. **9** (ml) Mark Richards/PhotoEdit, (bl) Sarah Hadley/Alamy, (br) Michael Newman/PhotoEdit. **10** (m) Artville, (b) Image Club Graphics. **17** (ml) Dynamic Graphics/Creatas/jupiterimages, (mr) Walter B. McKenzie/Getty Images, (bl) PhotoDisc/Getty Images, (br) Purestock/SuperStock. **19** Row 1: (l) PhotoDisc/Getty, Images, (lml) Janis Christie/Getty Images, (mr, r) Artville, (rmr) Liz Garza Williams. Row 2: (l) SuperStock, (m) John Paul Endress, (r) Getty Images. Row 3: (l) PhotoDisc/Getty Images, (m) Artville, (r) Liz Garza Williams. Row 4: (l) Digital Stock, (m, r) PhotoDisc/Getty Images. Row 5: (l) MetaTools, (m) John Paul Endress, (r) Liz Garza Williams. **20** Row 1: (l) Artville, (m) D. Falconer/PhotoLink/Getty Images, (r) PhotoDisc/Getty Images. Row 2: (l) Ron Chapple Stock/Photolibrary.com, (m) Stockbyte/Getty Images, (r) Liz Garza Williams. Row 3: (l) PhotoDisc/Getty Images, (m) Getty Images, (r) Liz Garza Williams. Row 4: (l) Liz Garza Williams, (m) Getty Images, (r) PhotoDisc/Getty Images. **21** (tl) moodboard/Corbis, (tr) Jose Luis Pelaez Inc/Blend Images/Corbis, (mr) Gabe Palmer/CORBIS, (br) Jon Feingersh/Blend Images/jupiterimages. **23** Row 1: (l) Liz Garza Williams, (r) D. Falconer/PhotoLink/Getty Images. Row 2: (l) Liz Garza Williams, (r) White Packert/Getty Images. Row 3: (l) Getty Images, (r) PhotoDisc/Getty Images. Row 4: (ml, mr) PhotoDisc/Getty Images, (r) D. Falconer/PhotoLink/Getty Images.

Row 5: (l) Artville, (ml, mr) Liz Garza Williams, (r) White Packert/Getty Images. **24** Row 1: (l) Artville, (r) Getty Images. Row 2: (l) Ron Chapple Stock/Photolibrary.com, (r) PhotoDisc/Getty Images. Row 3: (l) Liz Garza Williams, (r) D. Falconer/PhotoLink/Getty Images. Row 4: (l) Paul Beard/Getty Images, (ml) D. Falconer/PhotoLink/Getty Images, (mr, r) Liz Garza Williams. Row 5: (l) Digital Stock, (ml) Getty Images, (r) Liz Garza Williams. Row 6: (l, r) Liz Garza Williams, (ml) PhotoDisc/Getty Images, (mr) Stockbyte/Getty Images. **25** (ml) Image Source/SuperStock, (bl) BilderLounge/SuperStock, (mr) Peter Finger/Corbis. **33** (tl) Davis Barber/PhotoEdit, (tr) Nation Wong/Corbis, (ml) James Darell/Getty Images, (mr, br) BananaStock/jupiterimages, (bl) Getty Images. **34** (tl, tr, m, b) Liz Garza Williams. **35** Row 1: (l) Getty Images, (lml) Liz Garza Williams, (m) PhotoDisc/Getty Images, (rmr) Artville, (r) Liz Garza Williams. Row 2: (l) SuperStock, Inc./SuperStock, (ml) Corbis, (mr) Ryan McVay/Getty Images, (r) Alex Slobodkin/iStockphotos.com. Row 3: (l, ml) Artville, (mr) Getty Images, (r) John Paul Endress. Row 4: (l, mr) John Paul Endress, (ml) Getty Images, (r) Jack Fields/CORBIS. Row 5: (l, r) Artville, (ml) Getty Images, (mr) EyeWire. **36** Row 1: (l) John Paul Endress, (m) Artville, (r) Liz Garza Williams. Row 2: (l, m, r) Getty Images. Row 3: (l) Laura Dwight/CORBIS, (m) Liz Garza Williams, (r) D. Falconer/PhotoLink/Getty Images. Row 4: (l, r) PhotoDisc/Getty Images, (m) Getty Images. **37** (ml) Goodshoot/jupiterimages, (mr) Javier Larrea/age footstock, (bl) Sylvain Grandadam/age footstock, (br) Mike Kemp/Getty Images. **39** Row 1: (l) Liz Garza Williams, (m) Getty Images, (r) Laura Dwight/CORBIS. Row 2: (l) Getty Images, (m) PhotoDisc/Getty Images, (r) John Paul Endress. Row 3: (l, r) PhotoDisc/Getty Images, (m) D. Falconer/PhotoLink/Getty Images. Row 4: (l) Artville, (m) Thom Lang/Corbis. Row 5: (l) Getty Images, (m) PhotoDisc/Getty Images, (r) Liz Garza Williams. **40** Row 1: (l) Bill Aron/PhotoEdit, (m) PhotoDisc/Getty Images, (r) Liz Garza Williams. Row 2: (m) Getty Images, (r) C Square Studios/Getty Images. Row 3: (l) Laura Dwight/CORBIS, (m, r) Artville. Row 4: (l) Laura Dwight/CORBIS, (ml, r) PhotoDisc/Getty, Images, (mr) White Packert/Getty Images. Row 5: (l) D. Falconer/PhotoLink/Getty Images, (ml) Ryan McVay/Getty Images. Row 6: (l) Getty Images, (ml) PhotoDisc/Getty Images, (mr) C Square Studios/Getty Images, (r) Stockbyte/Getty Images. **41** (ml) STOCK4B-RF/Getty Images, (mr, bl, br) Alaska Stock. **49** (mr) Bob Daemmrich/PhotoEdit, (bl) Image Ideas/jupiterimages, (br) Siephoto/Masterfile. **51** (l) Image Library, (lml) Stockbyte/Getty Images, (m) Gavin Heiller/Getty Images, (rmr) PhotoDisc/Getty Images, (r) Digital Studio. **52** Row 1: (l) Laura Dwight/CORBIS, (m) John Paul Endress, (r) Liz Garza Williams. Row 2: (l) Liz Garza Williams, (m) John Paul Endress, (r) Getty Images.

Row 3: (l) Getty Images, (m) Artville, (r) Charles Krebs/Getty Images. Row 4: (l) Digital Studio, (m) Duomo/CORBIS, (r) Liz Garza Williams. **53** (all) Michael Newman/PhotoEdit. **55** Row 1: (l) C Square Studios/Getty Images, (ml, mr) Liz Garza Williams, (r) David Young-Wolff/PhotoEdit. Row 2: (l, m) Artville, (r) Getty Images. Row 3: (l) John Paul Endress, (m) PhotoDisc/Getty Images, (r) Getty Images. Row 4: (l, ml) Liz Garza Williams, (m) Artville, (r) David Young-Wolff/PhotoEdit. Row 5: (m, r) Liz Garza Williams. Row 6: (l) D. Falconer/PhotoLink/Getty Images, (m) Ryan McVay/Getty Images, (r) Laura Dwight/CORBIS. **56** Row 1: (l, ml) Liz Garza Williams, (m) Getty Images, (r) PhotoDisc/Getty Images. Row 2: (l) Getty Images, (m) Bill Aron/PhotoEdit, (r) D. Falconer/PhotoLink/Getty Images. Row 3: (l) PhotoDisc/Getty Images, (m) Laura Dwight/CORBIS, (r) Liz Garza Williams. Row 4: (l, m) Getty Images, (r) Duomo/CORBIS. Row 5: (l) Charles Krebs/Getty Images, (m) John Paul Endress, (r) Liz Garza Williams. Row 6: (l) David Young-Wolff/PhotoEdit, (m) Getty Images, (r) Artville. **57** (ml) Creatas/jupiterimages, (mr) Blend Images/SuperStock, (br) Myrleen Ferguson Cate/PhotoEdit. **65** (ml) Laurence Mouton/Photolibrary.com, (mr) Corbis/jupiterimages, (br) Rob Melnychuk/Brand X Pictures/jupiterimages. **67** (l) John Paul Endress, (ml, m) Getty Images, (mr) Artville, (r) Image Club Graphics. **68** Row 1: (l, m) PhotoDisc/Getty Images. Row 2: (l) Roger Ressmeyer/Corbis, (m) Liz Garza Williams, (r) Image Club Graphics. Row 3: (l) Siede Preis/Getty Images, (m) Liz Garza Williams, (r) Eyewire. Row 4: (l) John Paul Endress, (m) Liz Garza Williams. **69** (ml) Thinkstock/Corbis, (mr) PhotoDisc/Getty Images, (bl) Ingram Publishing/Superstock. **71** Row 1: (l) Getty Images, (m) PhotoDisc/Getty Images, (r) Image Club Graphics. Row 2: (l) Ryan McVay/Getty Images, (m) Liz Garza Williams, (r) Siede Preis/Getty Images. Row 3: (l) Bill Aron/PhotoEdit. Row 4: (l) Liz Garza Williams, (m) Roger Ressmeyer/Corbis, (r) PhotoDisc/Getty Images. Row 5: (l) Liz Garza Williams, (m) PhotoDisc/Getty Images, (r) D. Falconer/PhotoLink/Getty Images. **72** Row 1: (m) Bill Aron/PhotoEdit, (r) Getty Images. Row 2: (l) PhotoDisc/Getty Images, (m, r) Getty Images. Row 3: (l, r) PhotoDisc/Getty Images, (m) Getty Images. Row 4: (l) Liz Garza Williams, (ml) PhotoDisc/Getty Images, (mr) Roger Ressmeyer/Corbis, (r) Artville. Row 5: (l, m) Liz Garza Williams, (r) Siede Preis/Getty Images. Row 6: (l) Liz Garza Williams, (ml) Paul Beard/Getty Images, (mr) Image Club Graphics, (r) Getty Images. **73** (ml) Creatas/jupiterimages, (br) Digital Vision/Getty Images.

Illustrations:

11–12, 27–28, 43–44, 59–64, 75–76 Ben Shannon. **13–16, 29–32, 45–48, 77-80** Terry Julien.